READY, SET, GAME!

MW01137465

VIRTUAL GAMING

BY BETSY RATHBURN

oculus

BELLWETHER MEDIA • MINNEAPOLIS, MN

TM

TORQUE brims with excitement
perfect for thrill-seekers of all kinds.
Discover daring survival skills, explore
uncharted worlds, and marvel at mighty
engines and extreme sports. In *Torque* books,
anything can happen. Are you ready?

This edition first published in 2021 by Bellwether Media, Inc.

No part of this publication may be reproduced in whole or in part without
written permission of the publisher. For information regarding permission,
write to Bellwether Media, Inc., Attention: Permissions Department,
6012 Blue Circle Drive, Minnetonka, MN 55343.

Library of Congress Cataloging-in-Publication Data

Names: Rathburn, Betsy, author.
Title: Virtual reality gaming / by Betsy Rathburn.
Description: Minneapolis, MN : Bellwether Media Inc., 2021. | Series:
    Torque: Ready, Set, Game! | Includes bibliographical references and
    index. | Audience: Ages 7-12 | Audience: Grades 4-6 | Summary:
    "Amazing photography accompanies engaging information about
    virtual reality gaming. The combination of high-interest subject matter
    and light text is intended for students in grades 3 through 7"– Provided
    by publisher.
Identifiers: LCCN 2020048047 (print) | LCCN 2020048048 (ebook)
    | ISBN 9781644874592 | ISBN 9781648342523 (paperback) |
    ISBN 9781648341366 (ebook)
Subjects: LCSH: Video games–Juvenile literature. | Virtual
    reality–Juvenile literature.
Classification: LCC GV1469.3 .R36 2021 (print) | LCC GV1469.3
    (ebook) | DDC 794.8–dc23
LC record available at https://lccn.loc.gov/2020048047
LC ebook record available at https://lccn.loc.gov/2020048048

Editor: Elizabeth Neuenfeldt   Designer: Brittany McIntosh

Printed in the United States of America, North Mankato, MN.

TABLE OF CONTENTS

ROBOT RESCUE!

headset

You put on your **headset** and headphones. Now you are in the world of *ASTRO BOT Rescue Mission*! Which robot will you rescue first?

You use the controller to jump around. You blow into your headset's microphone. This spreads flower petals. Virtual reality makes you feel like you are in the game!

A SHORTER NAME

Virtual reality is often called VR.

ASTRO BOT
Rescue Mission

VIRTUAL REALITY GAMING
HISTORY

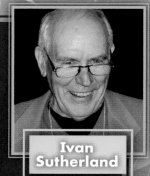

Ivan Sutherland

The Sword of Damocles was among the first VR headsets. Ivan Sutherland made it in 1968. It used **augmented reality** to place images over the real world!

VR continued to advance. By 1985, the VIEW headset used **CGI** to train astronauts! But VR was not yet used for games.

VIEW headset

VIRTUAL REALITY GAMING
TIMELINE

1968
The Sword of Damocles is one of the first VR headsets

1985
The VIEW headset uses CGI to train astronauts

1991
Virtuality brings VR to arcades

1994
Sega's VR-1 machines are available in arcades

1995
Nintendo Virtual Boy brings VR to handheld consoles

2012
The Oculus Rift is introduced and later released in 2016

2014
Google Cardboard brings VR to smartphones

2016
Sony's PlayStation VR is released

2019
Oculus Quest is released

SEGA

Sega released the VR-1 in 1994. Players wearing headsets sat in a machine. The machine moved along with the game!

VR came to **arcades** in the 1990s. Virtuality machines let players drive cars and battle robots. Players stood or sat in pods. They wore headsets and moved with joysticks or controllers.

In 1995, VR came to handheld consoles. Over twenty games were made for Nintendo's Virtual Boy. But **graphics** were limited. It could not track users' movements. The device was not successful.

Virtual Boy

The 2000s brought more advances. In 2012, the first Oculus Rift was introduced. It was connected to a powerful computer. **Sensors** tracked the movements of the headset and controllers. But people could not buy it until 2016.

Oculus Rift

HTC VIVE

The HTC Vive was made available in 2016. It was the first headset to let people freely walk around.

HTC Vive

In 2014, Google Cardboard brought VR to smartphones. Users put a smartphone into a cardboard headset. An **app** let people explore museums or drive through Paris.

Google Cardboard

VIRTUAL REALITY GAMING
TODAY

COMBO
232

Beat
Saber

80

Today, Oculus still makes VR headsets. The company released the Oculus Quest in 2019. It is completely wireless. Sensors are built in to the headset. Cameras help the headset track space as players move.

Oculus
Quest

Many gamers enjoy *Beat Saber* and *Ghost Giant. Superhot VR* and *Echo Arena* are popular, too!

POPULAR VIRTUAL REALITY GAMES
(BY NUMBER OF GAMES SOLD)

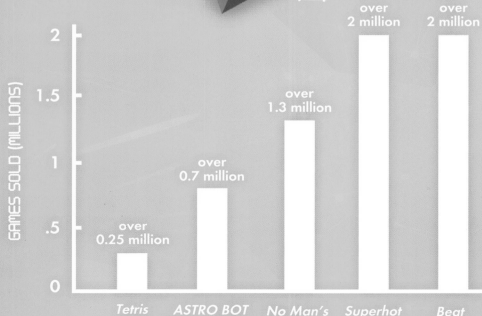

GAMES SOLD (MILLIONS)

over 2 million — Superhot VR

over 2 million — Beat Saber

over 1.3 million — No Man's Sky

over 0.7 million — ASTRO BOT Rescue Mission

over 0.25 million — Tetris Effect

GAMES

PlayStation also has a popular VR headset. Sony released the PlayStation VR for PlayStation 4 in 2016. Sensors and cameras tell the console where the player is moving.

PlayStation VR

More than 5 million PlayStation VR devices have been sold. Many players enjoy *Iron Man VR*, *Moss*, and *Tetris Effect*!

GAME SPOTLIGHT

GAME	*Iron Man VR*
YEAR	2020
TYPE	action
DEVICE	PlayStation VR
DESCRIPTION	Playing as Iron Man, players battle enemies and explore the world.

VR headsets make games more fun.
But they only use sight and hearing.
Future VR games may use more senses.

VIRTUAL REALITY HEADSETS
THROUGH TIME

2016
Oculus Rift

2016
HTC Vive

2016
PlayStation VR

2019
Oculus Rift S

2019
Oculus Quest

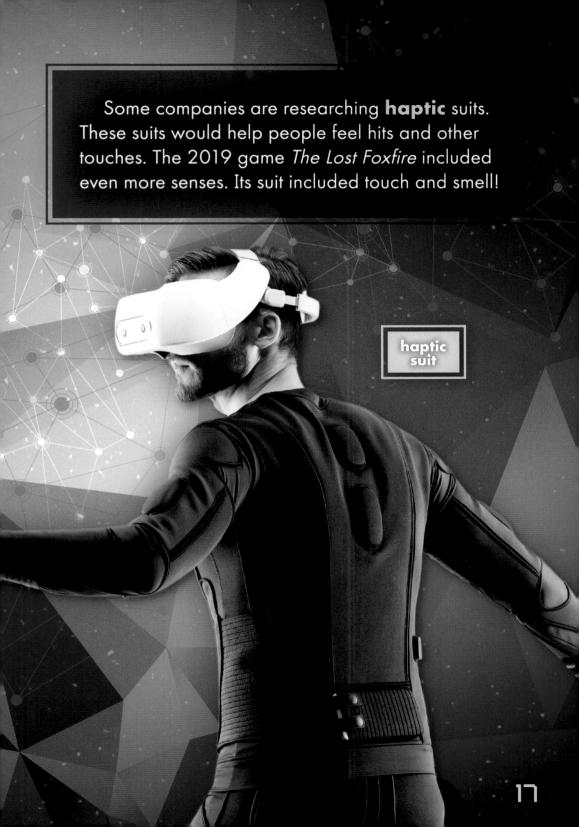

Some companies are researching **haptic** suits. These suits would help people feel hits and other touches. The 2019 game *The Lost Foxfire* included even more senses. Its suit included touch and smell!

haptic suit

THE VIRTUAL REALITY GAMING COMMUNITY

VR is an exciting new part of the video game community. People go to events to learn about new VR games. In 2018, the Classic Tetris World Championship let visitors try out *Tetris Effect*.

Tetris Effect

VR at E3

Some **conferences** honor the best games with awards. *Tetris Effect* won the Best VR/AR Game Award at the 2018 E3 conference!

Echo Arena

VIRTUAL REALITY GAMING
EVENT SPOTLIGHT

EVENT Rookie Rumble

GAME *Echo Arena*

HOST Collegiate VR Esports League

YEAR HELD 2020

DESCRIPTION Teams of four competed to become Echo Arena champions.

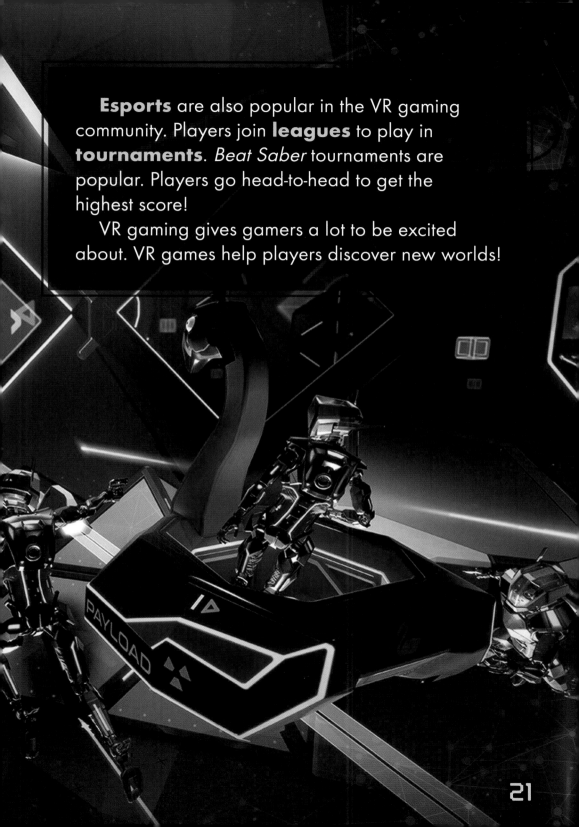

Esports are also popular in the VR gaming community. Players join leagues to play in tournaments. *Beat Saber* tournaments are popular. Players go head-to-head to get the highest score!

VR gaming gives gamers a lot to be excited about. VR games help players discover new worlds!

GLOSSARY

app—a program or game that can be downloaded onto mobile devices

arcades—places where people can go to play games

augmented reality—technology that places pictures or writing over images of the real world

CGI—artwork created by computers; CGI stands for computer-generated imagery.

conferences—events in which people gather to learn about a certain subject

esports—multiplayer video games that are played competitively for spectators

graphics—images displayed on a computer screen

haptic—related to touch; haptic suits make users feel like they are being touched.

headset—a helmet, visor, or other item a person wears on their head to experience VR

leagues—groups that come together to compete at a certain activity

sensors—small devices that measure something physical and react to it

tournaments—series of contests or games that make up competitions

TO LEARN MORE

AT THE LIBRARY

Challoner, Jack. *Virtual Reality*. New York, N.Y.: DK Publishing, 2017.

Gregory, Josh. *History of Esports*. Ann Arbor, Mich.: Cherry Lake Publishing, 2020.

Rathburn, Betsy. *Virtual Reality*. Minneapolis, Minn.: Bellwether Media, 2021.

ON THE WEB

FACTSURFER

Factsurfer.com gives you a safe, fun way to find more information.

1. Go to www.factsurfer.com.

2. Enter "virtual reality gaming" into the search box and click 🔍.

3. Select your book cover to see a list of related content.

INDEX